THE
SOLAR
SYSTEM

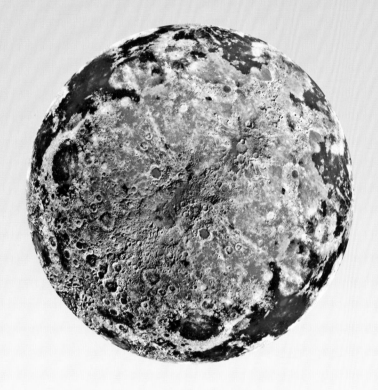

Chris Oxlade

HODDER
Wayland

An imprint of Hodder Children's Books

Titles in the *Science Files* series:

Electricity and Magnetism • Forces and Motion • Light and Sound • The Solar System

Science Files is a simplified and updated version of Hodder Wayland's
Science Fact Files.

**For more information on this series and other Hodder Wayland titles,
go to www.hodderwayland.co.uk**

Text copyright © Hodder Wayland 2005

Editor: Katie Sergeant
Designer: Simon Borrough
Typesetter: Victoria Webb
Illustrator: Alex Pang

First published in Great Britain in 1999 by Macdonald Young Books,
an imprint of Wayland Publishers Ltd
This edition updated and published in 2005 by Hodder Wayland,
an imprint of Hodder Children's Books

Oxlade, Chris
    The solar system. – (Science Files)
    1.Solar system – Juvenile literature
    I.Title
    523.2

ISBN 0750247096

Printed in China by WKT Company Ltd

Hodder Children's Books
A division of Hodder Headline Limited
338 Euston Road, London NW1 3BH

Cover picture: Earth with moon and star background.
Endpaper picture: The rings of the giant gas planet Saturn are a swarm of millions of tiny moons,
made of rock and ice.
Title page picture: The far side of the Moon.

We are grateful to the following for permission to reproduce photographs:
Getty Images/Digital Vision *cover* (Royalty-free); Science Photo Library 12–13 (NOAO), 14 top (NASA), 14 centre
(NASA), 17 (European Space Agency), 18 top (US Geological Survey), 19 bottom (NASA), 23 (NASA), 27 top (NASA),
29 (David A Hardy), 32 top (Detlev Van Ravenswaay), 32 bottom (François Gohier), 33 (Pekka Parviainen), 34
(European Space Agency). Remaining photos are courtesy of Digital Vision.

The website addresses (URLs) included in this book were valid at the time of going to press. However, because of the
nature of the Internet, it is possible that some addresses may have changed, or sites may have changed or closed down
since publication. While the author and Publishers regret any inconvenience this may cause the readers, no responsibility
for any such changes can be accepted by either the author or the Publisher.

Contents

Words in **bold** can be found in the glossary on page 44.

Introduction

Our **solar system** is made up of the Sun, nine planets, and dozens of moons. The planets move around the Sun and the moons move around their planets. There are many other smaller objects in the solar system, too. There are thousands of **asteroids** and **comets**, and millions of bits of dust and rock.

The four planets nearest the Sun, including the Earth, are small and rocky. The next four are much bigger, and made up of liquids and gases. Pluto, furthest from the Sun, has an icy surface.

Our galaxy is a great spiral 100,000 *light years* across. It contains about 100 billion stars.

Our solar system is just a tiny part of an enormous collection of stars, gas and dust, called a **galaxy**. Our Sun is not the only star in the galaxy with planets around it. In the last ten years we have found planets around other stars, too.

ORBITS AND GRAVITY

The planets move around the Sun, and the moons move around their planets, in paths called **orbits**. Most orbits are shaped like slightly squashed circles, called ellipses. The further a planet is from the Sun, the slower it moves, and the longer it takes to complete one orbit. The planets spin on their **axes** as they move around their orbits. The Sun spins on its axis, too.

Gravity is a force that pulls every object in the universe towards every other object. It holds the planets and moons in their orbits. For example, the pull of gravity between the Earth and the Sun keeps the Earth in orbit around the Sun;

Sun

The planets of our solar system.

Key	
1	Mercury
2	Venus
3	Earth
4	Mars
5	Jupiter
6	Saturn
7	Uranus
8	Neptune
9	Pluto

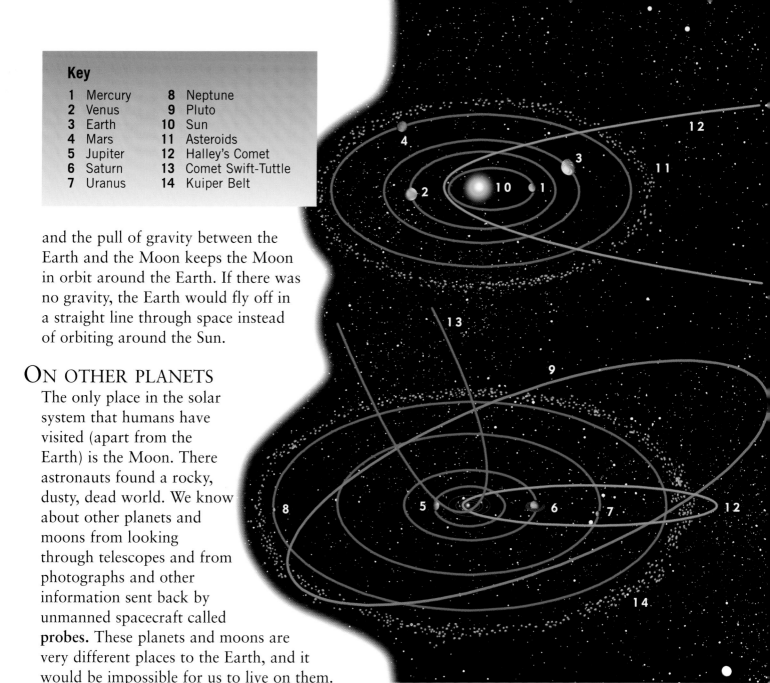

Key

1	Mercury	8	Neptune
2	Venus	9	Pluto
3	Earth	10	Sun
4	Mars	11	Asteroids
5	Jupiter	12	Halley's Comet
6	Saturn	13	Comet Swift-Tuttle
7	Uranus	14	Kuiper Belt

and the pull of gravity between the Earth and the Moon keeps the Moon in orbit around the Earth. If there was no gravity, the Earth would fly off in a straight line through space instead of orbiting around the Sun.

ON OTHER PLANETS

The only place in the solar system that humans have visited (apart from the Earth) is the Moon. There astronauts found a rocky, dusty, dead world. We know about other planets and moons from looking through telescopes and from photographs and other information sent back by unmanned spacecraft called **probes.** These planets and moons are very different places to the Earth, and it would be impossible for us to live on them.

Top: The inner part of the solar system. Bottom: The whole solar system. Pluto's orbit is tipped over and more squashed than the other planets. The comets (see pages 34-35) have very stretched orbits.

FACT FILE
SOLAR SYSTEM DATA

Number of planets:	9
Number of moons discovered:	more than a hundred
Diameter:	14,750 million kilometres
Distance from centre of galaxy:	30,000 light years*

* A light year is a unit of measurement in space. It is the distance light travels in a year, which is 9.46 million million kilometres.

The Birth of the Solar System

1. The solar system formed when a giant, swirling cloud of gas and dust was pulled together by its own gravity.

2. The Sun was born in the centre of the cloud. Clumps of cloud around it became the planets.

Astronomers think that the solar system formed about 4.6 billion (thousand million) years ago. The Sun, planets, moons, and all the other objects were made from a huge cloud of gas and dust. Gravity slowly pulled the gas and dust together. Eventually it turned into a spinning cloud with a very thick, dense centre. The centre of the cloud heated up because of collisions between the particles of gas and dust. It got so hot that **nuclear reactions** began, which created even more heat. This hot centre became a new star. The Sun was born.

Below: This is the Great Nebula in the *constellation* of Orion. New stars are being born here at the moment.

HOW THE PLANETS FORMED

The nuclear reactions that started in the Sun created bits of **atoms** called **sub-atomic particles**. These particles streamed away from the Sun, creating a solar 'wind'. The **solar wind** blew away much of the dust and gas in the cloud. But there was plenty of dust and gas left in a wide disc around the Sun. Gravity gradually made the dust and gas clump together, and over millions of years the planets formed. Smaller clumps of dust were trapped by the gravity of the planets, forming moons and rings around the planets.

FUTURE FILE

PLANETS ROUND OTHER STARS

Astronomers have found more than a hundred planets orbiting other stars in our galaxy. We can't see these planets with even the most powerful telescopes. From the Earth they look about the same size as a marble would on the Moon. We only know these moving planets exist because they make their stars wobble as they orbit round them, or make them dim when they pass in front of them. Nearly all these 'extrasolar' planets are **gas giants**, like Jupiter, but most astronomers think that Earth-like planets will be found one day.

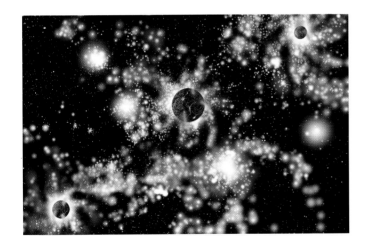

3. New planets of *molten* rock formed from the hot dust near the Sun.

4. The Sun will give out light and heat for another five billion years.

BITS LEFT OVER

Not all the dust from the original cloud ended up as part of the Sun, planets and moons. Some formed chunks of rock in all sorts of sizes. For hundreds of millions of years they crashed into the new planets and moons. We can still see the craters they made on other planets and the Moon.

The Sun

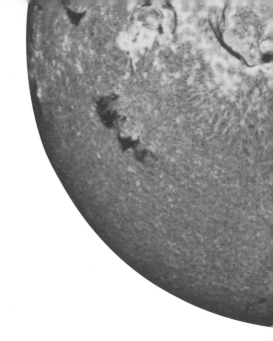

The Sun gives out an unimaginable amount of heat and light. Only a tiny fraction of this heat and light hits the Earth, but without it life would be impossible here. The Sun's enormous energy comes from nuclear reactions. They are the same reactions that happen in a nuclear bomb. The Sun is like a giant, ever-lasting nuclear explosion.

INSIDE THE SUN

The temperature in the Sun's **core** is 15 million °C. The pressure is 300 billion times the Earth's **atmospheric pressure**. At these extreme temperatures and pressures, atoms move at such high speed that their **nuclei** sometimes join together when they collide. This is called **nuclear fusion**, and it releases a huge amount of energy. In the Sun's core, hydrogen atoms fuse together to form helium atoms. An incredible 700 million tonnes of hydrogen is turned to helium every second.

Energy from the core travels to the surface of the Sun and then into space.

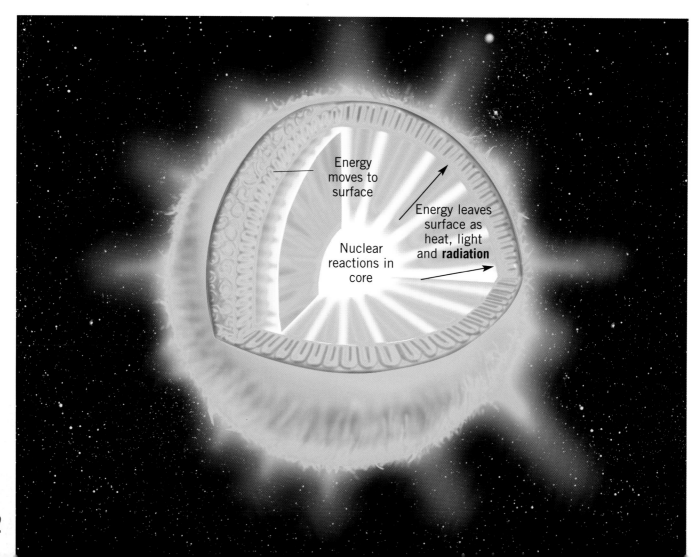

Energy moves to surface

Energy leaves surface as heat, light and **radiation**

Nuclear reactions in core

The dark red patches are sunspots on the surface of the Sun.

SURFACE FEATURES

The Sun's surface is a churning, violent place, made of hot gas. The temperature here is about 5.5 million °C. Some parts are not as bright as others, which makes the Sun look mottled. There are often darker spots on the surface called **sunspots**. They are hundreds or even thousands of kilometres across. Sunspots are places where the surface is cooler than everywhere else. They appear when heat from the Sun's core cannot reach the surface.

Sunspots come and go in a cycle. They get larger and more frequent and then die away again. The cycle takes about 11 years. Sunspots move as the Sun spins on its axis.

Solar flares are vast explosions that sometimes happen above sunspots. They last from a few minutes to a few hours, and give off radiation that can interfere with radios on the Earth.

A prominence is a tower or arch of glowing gas above the Sun's surface. Prominences can grow tens of thousands of kilometres high and last for months.

A prominence erupting from the Sun's surface.

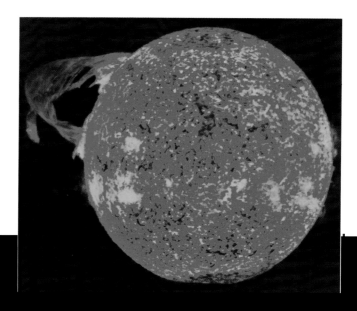

FACT FILE
SUN DATA

Rotation period:	26 days (equator); 37 days (poles)*
Diameter at equator:	1,392,000 km
Volume:	1,304,000 (Earth = 1)
Mass:**	1.99 billion billion billion tonnes = 329,000 x mass of Earth
Temperature:	5,500 ˚C (surface); approx. 15 million ˚C (centre)
Density:	1.41 (water = 1)
Gravity at surface:	27.9 (Earth = 1)

* The Sun spins faster at its equator than at its poles.
** This is the mass of the planet compared to the Earth

Mercury and Venus

Two planets are closer to the Sun than the Earth. Closest of all is Mercury, a planet not much bigger than our Moon. Venus is next. It is only slightly smaller than the Earth. Both planets have bare, rocky surfaces.

LONG DAYS AND NIGHTS

A year is the time it takes a planet to complete one orbit of the Sun. Mercury's year lasts for just 88 Earth days. But Mercury spins on its axis very slowly. One complete rotation lasts for nearly 59 Earth days, compared with one day for Earth. The result is that on Mercury, daylight and night-time both last for 88 days each.

Mercury's *meteorite* craters were made billions of years ago.

Swirling clouds of sulphuric acid hide Venus's surface.

Mercury has no atmosphere to protect it from the Sun. During its long day, the surface is baked until it reaches 420 °C. During the long night the temperature can fall to –180 °C. The surface is covered with meteorite craters.

GREENHOUSE PLANET

Venus is twice as far from the Sun as Mercury, but its surface gets even hotter than Mercury's. The planet has an atmosphere of thick carbon dioxide gas. The gas traps heat from the Sun like a greenhouse, raising the surface temperature up to 740 °C. The atmospheric pressure is ninety times higher than on Earth. We can't see the surface because the atmosphere is full of clouds of sulphuric acid.

Space probes have landed on Venus and taken photographs, but have been put out of action in minutes by the pressure and temperature. However, Venus's surface has been revealed using **radar** on probes in orbit around the planet. There are towering mountains, flat plains and craters.

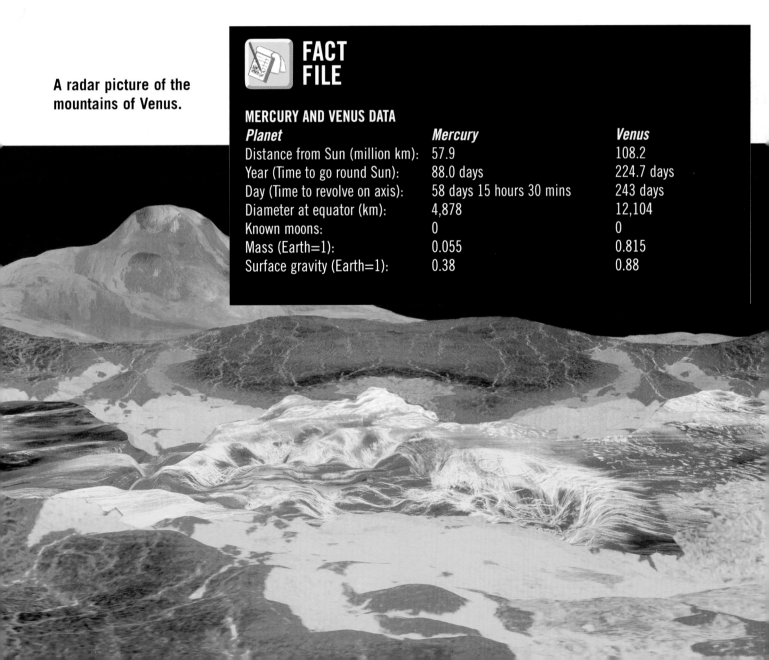

A radar picture of the mountains of Venus.

FACT FILE

MERCURY AND VENUS DATA

Planet	Mercury	Venus
Distance from Sun (million km):	57.9	108.2
Year (Time to go round Sun):	88.0 days	224.7 days
Day (Time to revolve on axis):	58 days 15 hours 30 mins	243 days
Diameter at equator (km):	4,878	12,104
Known moons:	0	0
Mass (Earth=1):	0.055	0.815
Surface gravity (Earth=1):	0.38	0.88

Earth

Our planet, the Earth, is a very special place. It is close enough to the Sun to get plenty of heat and light. But the Earth is not so close to the Sun that it bakes, like Mercury. The atmosphere traps the heat, but not so much as on Venus. This allows water to exist as a liquid over most of the surface. On other planets it would freeze or boil. All these factors make it possible for life to flourish on Earth.

INSIDE THE EARTH

The Earth is made up of four layers. We live on the thin, rocky outer layer, called the **crust.** Underneath the crust is the thickest layer, called the **mantle,** which is made up of rock. The top layer, called the upper mantle, is so hot that the rock is slightly molten, like a treacly liquid. Heat from the centre of the Earth makes this rock swirl about very slowly. The lower mantle is made from hot rock. Under the mantle is the core, which is made of iron and nickel. The core's temperature is about 4,500 °C.

HISTORY FILE

LIFE ON EARTH

Millions of years ago

4,600	Earth formed
3,800	Very simple life starts in the oceans
500	First fish appear
400	First plants appear
380	Some animals move from sea to land
350	First reptiles appear
280	First insects appear
225	First mammals appear
200	First birds appear
65	Dinosaurs die out
1.5	First humans appear

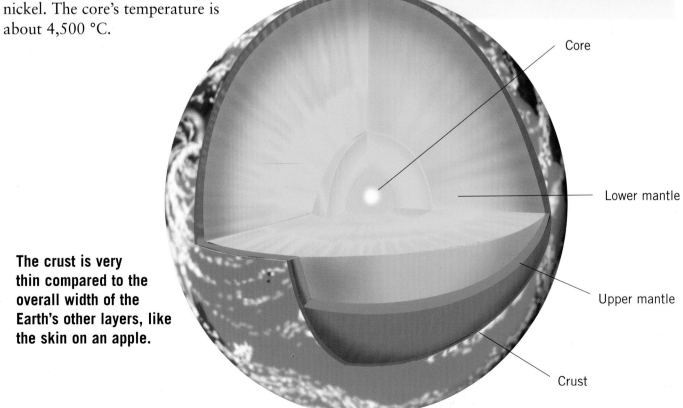

Core

Lower mantle

Upper mantle

Crust

The crust is very thin compared to the overall width of the Earth's other layers, like the skin on an apple.

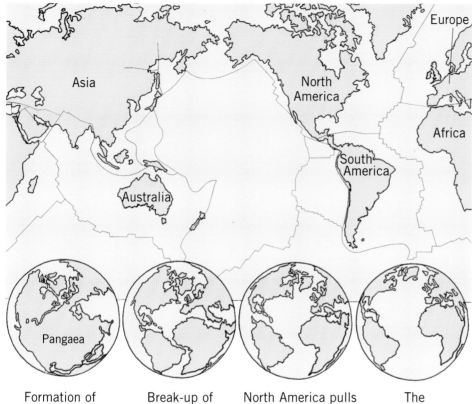

Asia

North America

Europe

Africa

South America

Australia

Pangaea

The red lines are the edges of the crust's plates. The plates slowly shrink, grow and change shape. There was just one continent, called Pangaea, 180 million years ago.

Formation of Pangaea, 250 million years ago

Break-up of Pangaea, 180 million years ago

North America pulls away from Europe, 70 million years ago

The continents today

Two-thirds of the Earth is covered with liquid water.

EARTH'S CRUST

Underneath the oceans the crust is 5-10 kilometres thick. Under the continents it is 20-70 kilometres thick. The crust is cracked into giant pieces called **tectonic plates**. The swirling rock in the upper mantle makes the plates drift slowly about. In some places they move apart and in others they collide, pushing up mountain ranges.

FACT FILE

EARTH DATA

Distance from Sun (million km): 149.6
Year (Time to go round Sun): 365.26 d
Day (Time to revolve on axis): 23 h 56 m
Diameter at Equator (km): 12,756
Known moons: 1
Mass (Earth=1): 1 (= 5,980 billion billion tonnes)
Surface gravity (Earth=1): 1 (= 9.81 metres per second per second)

Mars

Of all the planets in the solar system, Mars is the most like the Earth. It has a rocky surface of deserts, valleys, mountains and volcanoes, and also ice caps. A Martian day is only a bit shorter than an Earth day. Mars is called the Red Planet because its rocks are a reddy-brown colour. They contain iron oxide, or rust.

ICE CAPS AND ATMOSPHERE

Mars has frozen ice caps at its poles. The ice here is made from frozen water and frozen carbon dioxide. During the Martian summer the ice begins to disappear. It doesn't turn to liquid, but instead turns straight to gas in the atmosphere. Mars has a very thin atmosphere mostly made up of carbon dioxide.

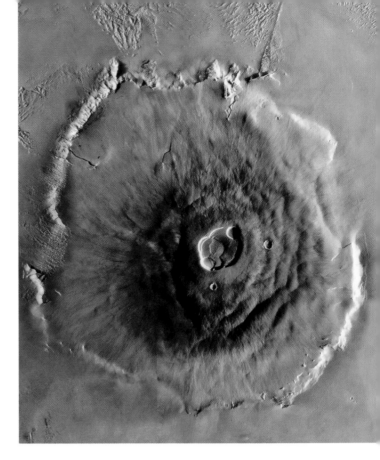

Looking down on the enormous Martian volcano, Olympus Mons.

Giant valleys and canyons stretching across the Martian surface.

TEST FILE

WATCHING MARS

Mars looks like a red star in the night sky. It is brightest in the months before and after opposition (when it is nearest to the Earth). Here are the opposition dates and the constellations (groups of stars) where Mars can be seen. You can see the constellations on a star map.

2005	7 November	Aries
2007	25 December	Gemini
2010	30 January	Cancer
2012	4 March	Leo
2014	9 April	Virgo

VALLEYS AND MOUNTAINS

There is a huge system of valleys on Mars called the Valles Marineris. The system is 4,000 kilometres long, 700 kilometres across and 7 kilometres deep. It makes Earth's Grand Canyon, in Arizona, USA, look like a tiny scratch! These valleys must have been made by flowing water. Scientists think the water emerged when underground ice was melted by erupting volcanoes.

Mars also has the biggest mountain in the solar system. It is an **extinct** volcano called Olympus Mons. It is 27 kilometres high – that's three times higher than the tallest volcano on Earth.

LIFE ON MARS

Because there is water on Mars, scientists think that life could have existed there in the past. Simple life forms may even exist under the ice caps today. Several probes have searched Martian rocks and the Martian atmosphere for signs of life, but so far have found no firm evidence.

Mars is just over half the width of Earth.

FACT FILE

MARS DATA

Distance from Sun (million km):	227.9
Year (Time to go round Sun):	687.0 d
Day (Time to revolve on axis):	24 h 37 m
Diameter at equator (km):	6,794
Known moons:	2
Mass (Earth=1):	0.11
Surface gravity (Earth=1):	0.38

A view of the rocky surface of Mars, taken by a Viking lander.

Asteroids

An asteroid is a small lump of rock that orbits the Sun. Asteroids are also known as minor planets. There are thousands of asteroids in the solar system. Most are in a ring between the orbits of Mars and Jupiter, called the **asteroid belt**. These asteroids are thought to be bits of rock that never clumped together to make a planet when the solar system was formed.

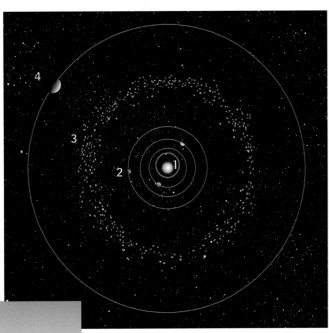

The asteroid belt is between Mars and Jupiter.

Key

1 Sun
2 Mars
3 Asteroid belt
4 Jupiter

COUNTING ASTEROIDS

The first asteroid ever discovered, called Ceres, was seen in 1801 by Italian astronomer Giuseppe Piazzi. Ceres is 940 kilometres across, and is still the biggest asteroid we know about. Three more asteroids, called Pallas, Vesta and Juno, had been discovered by 1807. No more asteroids were found until 1845. Since then new asteroids have been discovered every year.

TEST FILE

SEARCHING FOR ASTEROIDS

Before the asteroids were discovered, astronomers thought there was a small planet between Mars and Jupiter. They thought this because of the Titius-Bode rule, named after two German astronomers. The rule states that if the distance from the Sun to the Earth is set at 10 units, then the distances from the Sun to the planets up to Uranus (which was the last planet known then) should be 4, 7, 10, 16, 28, 52, 100, 196 units. The figures almost matched the true distances to Mercury, but there was no planet at distance 28.

Planet	True distance	Titius-Bode rule distance
Mercury	4	4
Venus	7	7
Earth	10	10
Mars	15	16
		28
Jupiter	52	52
Saturn	95	100
Uranus	192	196

In 1800 a group of astronomers joined forces to try to find the missing planet. They called themselves the Celestial Police. But instead of finding a planet they found three asteroids.

Astronomers have worked out the orbits of several thousand of these asteroids, so that we know where each one is all the time and won't mistake it for a new one.

If a giant asteroid hit the Earth the human race would be wiped out.

us so that warnings can be given. In 2004 an asteroid 30 metres across whizzed by just 40,000 kilometres from Earth.

The asteroid Vesta is 555 kilometres across and covered in craters made by meteorites.

SMALL BUT DEADLY

Asteroids are small compared to the 'major' planets such as Earth and Mars. If all the thousands of asteroids were put together they would make up less than a tenth of our Moon. They are too small for gravity to pull them into spheres like the major planets. Instead they are shapeless lumps, like giant potatoes.

Although most asteroids stay in the asteroid belt, some move in orbits that bring them closer to the Sun. Sometimes they pass close to the Earth. A collision could be catastrophic, so the Near-Earth Object Program searches for asteroids that could hit

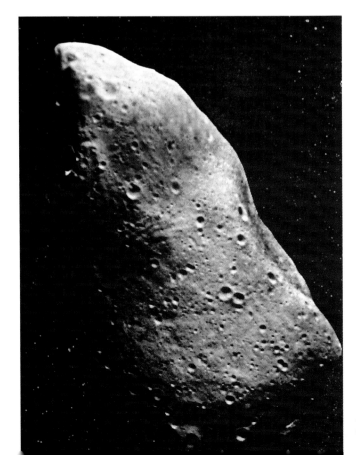

Jupiter

Jupiter is the biggest planet in our solar system. Jupiter is a massive ball made mostly of hydrogen. Hydrogen is normally a gas on Earth, which is why Jupiter is called a gas giant. The planet's surface of liquid hydrogen is hidden by the cloudy atmosphere, which is made up of hydrogen with some helium, methane and ammonia. The clouds form dark and light bands around the planet, with giant storms wider than the Earth. The biggest storm of all can be seen through telescopes on Earth. It is called the Great Red Spot.

More than 1,300 Earths could fit inside Jupiter.

TEST FILE

WATCHING JUPITER

Jupiter is brightest in the months before and after opposition. Here are the opposition dates and the constellations where Jupiter can be seen:

2006	5 May	Libra
2007	6 June	Scorpio
2008	9 July	Sagittarius
2009	15 August	Capricorn
2010	21 September	Pisces
2011	29 October	Aries
2012	3 December	Taurus

SPINNING FAST

Jupiter is 318 times larger than the Earth, and more massive than all the other planets put together. But it spins very quickly. A Jupiter day lasts a bit less than 10 Earth hours. It spins so fast that the surface spreads outwards around its equator. If you observe Jupiter through a telescope you can see the bulge.

FACT FILE

JUPITER DATA

Distance from Sun (million km):	778
Year (Time to go round Sun):	11.9 y
Day (Time to revolve on axis):	9 h 50 m
Diameter at equator (km):	142,984
Known moons:	more than 60
Mass (Earth=1):	317.8
Surface gravity (Earth=1):	2.6

Jupiter's Great Red Spot is a storm that has lasted for centuries.

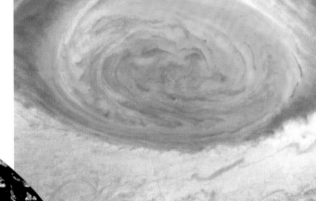

Gaseous hydrogen

Core of rock and iron

Solid hydrogen

Liquid hydrogen

The immense pressure inside Jupiter keeps hydrogen solid inside.

INSIDE JUPITER

Jupiter's atmosphere is about 1,000 kilometres deep. Underneath it the pressure is so high that the hydrogen turns to liquid. Deeper down, the hydrogen becomes solid, like metal. The planet's small core is probably made of rock and iron. The temperature in the core is thought to be more than 20,000 °C. That's hotter than the centre of the Sun.

Saturn

Saturn is the second largest planet in the solar system. Like the biggest planet, Jupiter, it is a gas giant made almost completely of hydrogen. Saturn's most famous features are its rings, which are the widest and brightest rings in the whole solar system.

A WORLD OF RINGS

Saturn's spectacular rings are easily visible through small telescopes from Earth. From here we can see three rings, which look solid. There also appears to be a wide gap between two of them, called the Cassini division.

When the space probe Voyager 1 flew past Saturn in 1980 it sent back the first close-up photographs of the rings. The photographs showed that the rings are not solid, but are made up of millions of orbiting chunks

WATCHING SATURN

Saturn is brightest every year and 13 days. It looks like a bright yellow star. Here are the opposition dates and the constellations where Saturn can be seen. Every 15 years we see Saturn's rings edge-on. At other times they are opened out.

2006	28 January	Cancer
2007	10 February	Leo
2008	24 February	Leo
2009	9 March	Leo
2010	22 March	Virgo
2011	4 April	Virgo
2012	16 April	Virgo

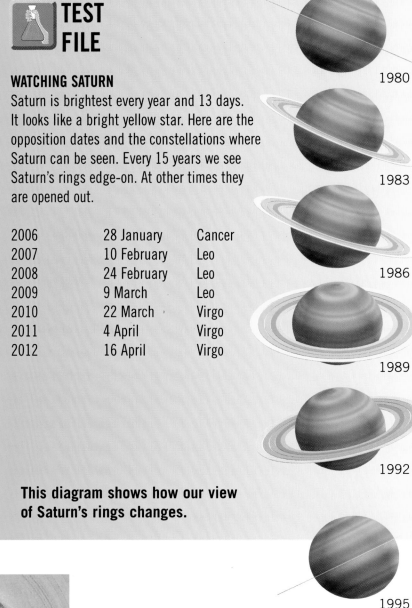

This diagram shows how our view of Saturn's rings changes.

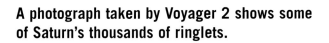

A photograph taken by Voyager 2 shows some of Saturn's thousands of ringlets.

of rock and ice. They also showed that each ring is made up of thousands of smaller rings, called **ringlets.** Probes also discovered several more rings, including a faint ring 300,000 kilometres across.

FACT FILE

SATURN DATA

Distance from Sun (million km):	1,427
Year (Time to go round Sun):	29.5 y
Day (Time to revolve on axis):	10 h 14 m
Diameter at equator (km):	120,536
Known moons:	more than 30
Mass (Earth=1):	95.1
Surface gravity (Earth=1):	1.15

INSIDE AND OUTSIDE

At the centre of Saturn there is a solid core of rock. Here the temperature is about 15,000 °C. Outside the core is a layer of solid hydrogen that stretches about halfway to the surface. Next comes a layer of liquid hydrogen right up to the surface. Saturn is very light compared to its huge size. It would just float in water. Above the surface is an atmosphere of hydrogen and helium gases. Violent winds blow through the atmosphere.

Saturn's middle bulges out as the planet spins.

1997

2000

2003

2006

2009

FUTURE FILE

THE CASSINI MISSION

The Cassini spacecraft was launched in 1997. It arrived in orbit around Saturn in 2004. It will stay for four years, sending back to Earth information about Saturn, its rings and moons. Cassini is carrying a probe called Huygens, designed to land on one of Saturn's moons, Titan.

Uranus and Neptune

Uranus and Neptune are both gas giants. Uranus is nearly twenty times further from the Sun than the Earth. It takes more than 84 Earth years to complete its orbit. Uranus was discovered in 1781 by German astronomer William Herschel. It was the first new planet to be found for two thousand years. Uranus has nine thin rings made of very dark boulders.

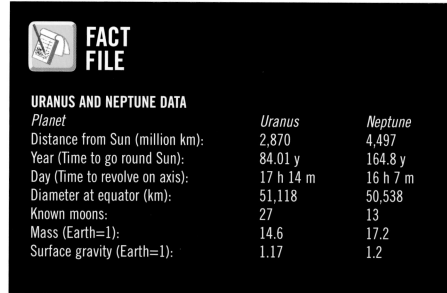

FACT FILE

URANUS AND NEPTUNE DATA

Planet	Uranus	Neptune
Distance from Sun (million km):	2,870	4,497
Year (Time to go round Sun):	84.01 y	164.8 y
Day (Time to revolve on axis):	17 h 14 m	16 h 7 m
Diameter at equator (km):	51,118	50,538
Known moons:	27	13
Mass (Earth=1):	14.6	17.2
Surface gravity (Earth=1):	1.17	1.2

Key

1 Uranus
2 Miranda
3 Ariel
4 Umbriel
5 Titania
6 Oberon

← Orbit of Uranus around the Sun

The moons of Uranus orbit at right angles to the orbit of Uranus around the Sun.

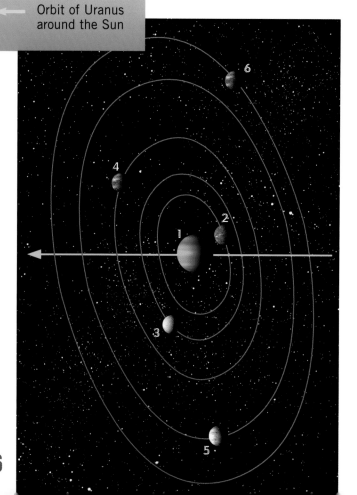

PLANET ON EDGE

Most of the planets stand almost upright as they orbit the Sun. But Uranus is tilted right over on its side. This means that each of its poles is in sunlight for half the orbit and in darkness for half the orbit. Uranus has hardly any visible features. The greeny-blue atmosphere is made up mainly of hydrogen. Underneath the atmosphere is a giant sea of ammonia, water and methane. In the centre is a core of rock.

THE BLUE PLANET

Neptune is about thirty times further from the Sun than the Earth. It takes 165 Earth years to complete one orbit of the Sun. Neptune is almost the same size as Uranus, but it looks more blue.

Inside, Neptune is very similar to Uranus, with a rocky core, a layer of liquid and a thick atmosphere. Hardly any heat from the Sun reaches this far out into the solar system. It is heat from the centre of Neptune that warms its atmosphere, making super-strong winds blow around the planet. An enormous storm, called the Great Dark Spot, rages in the atmosphere.

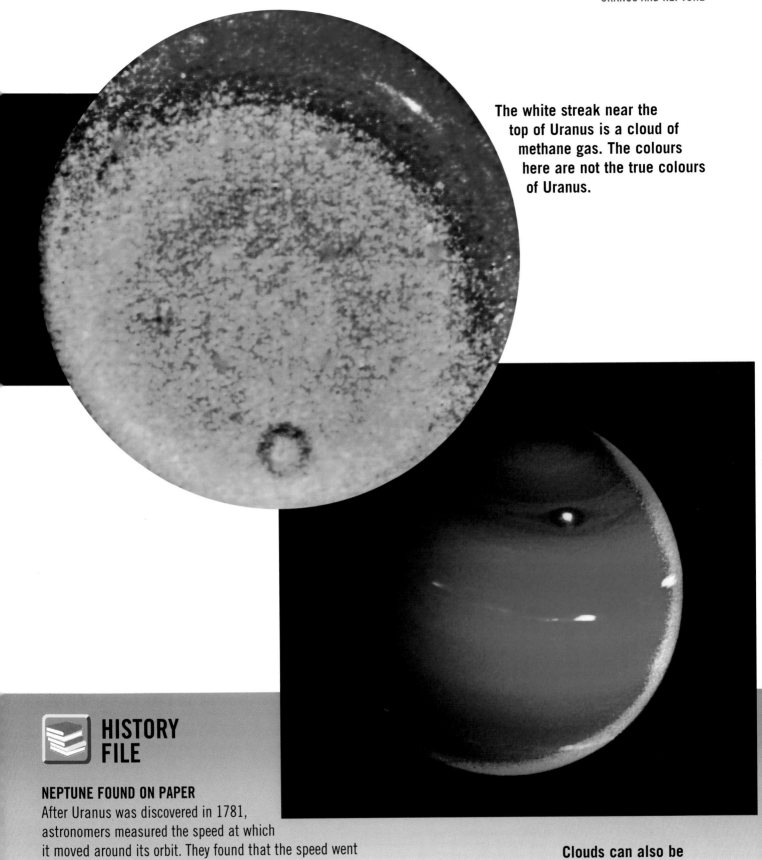

The white streak near the top of Uranus is a cloud of methane gas. The colours here are not the true colours of Uranus.

Clouds can also be seen on Neptune.

HISTORY FILE

NEPTUNE FOUND ON PAPER

After Uranus was discovered in 1781, astronomers measured the speed at which it moved around its orbit. They found that the speed went up and down slightly. Some thought that the orbit was being disturbed by the gravity of another planet that nobody knew about. In 1845 two mathematicians calculated where this unknown planet would be if it actually existed. Astronomers began searching with their telescopes, and Neptune was found in 1846.

27

Pluto and Beyond

Pluto was discovered in 1930. It is normally thought of as the last of the nine planets in the solar system, but it is very different to the other planets. It is made of rock and ice and is smaller than many of the solar system's moons. Its orbit is also very stretched. Some of the time it is outside Neptune's orbit, and some of the time it is inside. We now know that Pluto is just one of dozens of small icy objects in the area. So some astronomers no longer think of Pluto as a proper planet like the other eight.

HISTORY FILE

THE WRONG PLANET

A hundred years ago, astronomers decided that there must be another planet beyond Neptune. One of them, Percival Lowell, worked out how big it should be and where it should be. Unfortunately he couldn't find it. Another astronomer, Clyde Tombaugh, started searching after Lowell's death. In 1930 he found Pluto almost where Lowell had predicted. But Pluto was much smaller than Lowell's calculations showed. Modern astronomers don't think Lowell's planet actually exists.

THE DOUBLE PLANET

Pluto has one moon, called Charon. Charon is about half as wide as Pluto, and much closer to it than Earth is to the Moon. Pluto and Charon orbit round each other, forming a 'double' planet. Charon was discovered in 1978 after an American astronomer, Jim Christy, noticed that Pluto looked pear-shaped through a telescope. He realised that he was seeing two objects very close together. Pluto is the only planet never visited by a space probe, and it is so far away and so small that it is impossible to see much surface detail through telescopes on Earth.

Pluto's surface might look like this.

PLUTO DATA

Distance from Sun (million km):	5,900
Year (Time to go round Sun):	247.7 y
Day (Time to revolve on axis):	6 d 9 h 18 m
Diameter at equator (km):	2,324
Known moons:	1
Mass (Earth=1):	0.002
Surface gravity (Earth=1):	0.06

This is what astronomers think Pluto and Charon look like.

THE KUIPER BELT

The Kuiper Belt is a ring of objects that orbits the Sun further out than Neptune. In the 1950s two astronomers, Kenneth Essex Edgeworth and Gerard Kuiper, suggested that these objects existed. But it took until 1992 for the first **Kuiper Belt Object (KBO)** to be found. Since then many hundreds of KBOs have been discovered. They are thought to be made of **matter** left over from the formation of the solar system. Some comets are thought to come from the Kuiper Belt.

Many KBOs have similar orbits to Pluto, and so are called Plutinos, which means 'little Plutos'. Some KBOs are bigger than Pluto. This is why some astronomers think of Pluto and Charon as KBOs rather than a planet and moon system. There are probably many thousands of KBOs waiting to be discovered. Astronomers think that if all the KBOs were put together they would make a single planet as big as Earth. We will have to wait until a probe visits to find out more about this part of the solar system.

Moons

Moons are objects that orbit round planets. Moons are sometimes called **satellites.** The four rocky planets in the inner solar system have only a few moons between them. Mercury and Venus have no moons. Earth has just one – the Moon – and Mars has two tiny moons. Things are very different in the outer solar system. Each of the gas giants has a whole family of moons, and more moons are found every year. Jupiter has more than sixty moons and Saturn has more than thirty. Uranus has twenty-seven moons and Neptune has thirteen moons.

Europa (Jupiter)

Io (Jupiter)

Triton (Neptune)

Ganymede (Jupiter)

Moon (Earth)

Callisto (Jupiter)

Titan (Saturn)

The solar system's biggest moons.

JUPITER'S MOONS

Jupiter's moons were made in two different ways. Some of the moons, including the four biggest ones, were formed at the same time as the planet itself. They orbit in the same direction that the planet spins. The other moons are lumps of rock and ice that flew close to Jupiter and were captured by its powerful gravity. Some orbit in the opposite direction.

DIFFERENT WORLDS

Jupiter's four biggest moons, called Io, Europa, Ganymede and Callisto, show how even the moons of the same planets can be very different worlds. Active volcanoes erupt on Io. The surface is covered with red and orange patches of sulphur. Europa is quite

The nine largest moons of Saturn. Iapetus and Phoebe are shown separately because they are so far from Saturn.

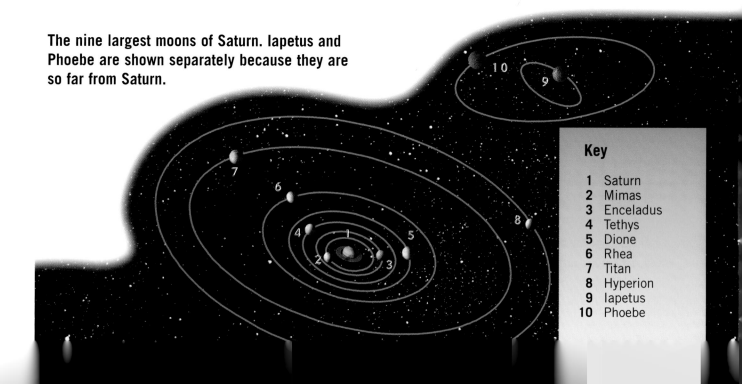

Key

1	Saturn
2	Mimas
3	Enceladus
4	Tethys
5	Dione
6	Rhea
7	Titan
8	Hyperion
9	Iapetus
10	Phoebe

A close-up image of Jupiter's moon Io. A volcano is erupting on the horizon.

different. It is covered with a smooth layer of ice that could be 100 kilometres thick. Underneath could be liquid water, where astronomers think that simple life could have developed. Ganymede and Callisto have icy surfaces pitted with craters. Ganymede is the solar system's largest moon.

TITAN

Saturn's largest moon is called Titan. It is the only moon in the solar system with an atmosphere, which is thick and made mostly of nitrogen. Scientists think that the atmosphere and surface of Titan might be like the Earth was soon after it formed.

 FUTURE FILE

DEATH OF A MOON
Moons don't stay in the same orbit for ever. Our Moon is very slowly moving away from the Earth. One of Neptune's moons, Triton, is very gradually spiralling inwards. Eventually it will break up to become a ring around Neptune.

Meteors and Meteorites

If you watch the night sky for a few minutes you might see a tiny streak of light called a shooting star. The proper name for a shooting star is a **meteor**. A meteor appears when a grain of dust falls into the Earth's atmosphere at immense speed and burns up because of friction with the air.

A thin slice of a meteorite that fell to the ground in Chile.

 FACT FILE

METEOR AND METEORITE DATA

About 1,000 tonnes of dust falls into the atmosphere from space every day.

•

The heaviest *meteor shower* was the Leonids of 1966. On 17 November that year 60,000 meteors were seen every hour.

•

The largest meteorite ever found weighs 59 tonnes. It fell thousands of years ago in Namibia.

•

The best-preserved meteorite crater is Meteor Crater in Arizona, USA. It is 1.26 kilometres across and 175 metres deep.

Meteor Crater in Arizona, USA, was formed about 27,000 years ago.

METEOR SHOWERS

On most nights of the year we see only a few meteors. But at certain times there are hundreds or even thousands of meteors every hour. These events are called meteor showers. They gradually build up and then steadily die away. They happen when the Earth passes through a trail of dust left by a comet. Some meteor showers always happen on the same day every year. For example, there is always a meteor shower on 4 May when the Earth goes through the dust trail of Halley's Comet.

METEORITES

Sometimes larger chunks of rock hurtle into the Earth's atmosphere. They probably come from asteroids that have broken up in collisions. Like meteors, the rocks burn up because of friction. But the bigger ones do not burn up completely. The bits of rock left over that hit the ground are called meteorites. Some are stony and some are like lumps of metal. When big meteorites land they blast craters in the ground. The Moon is covered with craters, so it is likely that millions of meteorites hit the Earth in the past too, but their craters have now eroded away.

A streak of light made by a meteor glowing white hot as it enters the Earth's atmosphere.

TEST FILE

MAJOR METEOR SHOWERS

All the meteor showers that return every year are given names. They are named after the object in the night sky that they appear to come from. Meteor showers appear on the same dates each year. Here are the names of the biggest meteor showers:

Date	Name of shower	Constellation where meteors seem to come from
3 January	Quadrantids	Boötes (there used to be a constellation here called The Quadrant)
4 May	Eta Aquarids	Aquarius (near star Eta Aquarii)
11 August	Perseids	Perseus
20 October	Orionids	Orion
16 November	Leonids	Leo
13 December	Geminids	Gemini

Comets

Gas and dust pouring from the nucleus of Halley's Comet.

A comet is one of the most spectacular displays seen in the night sky. If a comet comes into the inner solar system, it grows tails of gas and dust. The tails can stretch across millions of kilometres of space. As the comet moves away again, the tails shrink and disappear.

Most comets only visit the inner solar system once and are never seen again. But some are trapped in orbit around the Sun in very squashed orbits. They appear in the sky again and again, always with the same gap between each visit. But they spend most of their time far from us in the outer solar system.

Halley's Comet appears every 76 years. Its orbit takes it closer to the Sun than the Earth. Then it moves away again, going beyond Neptune before it starts to come back. Comet Hale-Bopp has a much longer orbit than Halley. It was visible in 1998, but it won't return until the year 4350.

FACT FILE

HALLEY'S COMET
When Halley's Comet visited in 1986, the Giotto probe went to meet it. Photographs showed that Halley is a potato-shaped lump about 16 kilometres long. In 2004 the Stardust probe collected gas and dust from the tail of comet Wild-2. It will bring the samples back to Earth for analysis.

The orbit of Halley's Comet. A comet's tail always points away from the Sun.

Key
1 Tail lengthens as comet approaches Sun
2 Tail longest closest to Sun
3 Tail shrinks as comet moves away from Sun
→ Path of comet

HISTORY FILE

COMET TALES

• Halley's Comet is named after Edmond Halley. In 1705 Halley realised that many comet sightings from history were all 76 years apart, and that they must be the same comet returning.

• Comet Encke takes just three years and four months to complete its orbit. It has been seen from Earth dozens of times.

• The Great Comet, which was seen in 1843, had a tail 330 million kilometres long. It would have stretched from the Earth to the Sun and back.

• Some comets have enormous orbits. Astronomers estimate that Delavan's Comet, seen in 1914, will not be seen again for another 24 million years.

• Comets can collide with other bodies in space. In 1998 the SOHO probe photographed two comets crashing into the Sun.

• Comets have collided with the Earth in the past. In 1908 a comet landed and exploded in Siberia, knocking down trees for 600 kilometres around.

COMETS CLOSE-UP

The solid part of a comet is called its nucleus. It is like a huge dirty snowball. It is made up of bits of rock and ice. When a comet moves closer to the Sun than Jupiter, the Sun's heat turns the ice on the surface of the nucleus to gas. Gas and dust stream from the surface. They spread out into a cloud called a corona. The solar wind, made up of particles moving away from the Sun, carries the gas and dust away, forming two tails, one of gas and one of dust.

WHERE COMETS COME FROM

Astronomers think that all comets come from one of two places. One is the Kuiper Belt, a ring of icy objects outside the orbit of Neptune (see page 29). The other is a giant cloud of comets far outside the orbit of Pluto. This is called the Oort Cloud. It could stretch two light years into space, and could contain billions of comets.

Halley's Comet, photographed in 1986 on its last visit.

Exploring the Solar System

Human beings have only explored a tiny amount of the solar system. The first person to go into space was a Russian cosmonaut called Yuri Gagarin. He orbited the Earth a few times in 1961. In 1969 astronauts landed on the Moon for the first time. Five more missions went to the Moon, the last in 1972. The astronauts explored the Moon's surface and brought back samples of Moon rock to Earth.

Since 1972 no humans have gone further than Earth orbit, although the USA plans to return to the Moon in the future. It is much easier to send small robot spacecraft called probes out into the solar system instead. Journeys to the other planets can take many years, and humans could not survive in some of the places probes visit.

The Voyager probes took the first close-up photographs of Saturn's rings.

A Titan II rocket lifting off. On top is a Gemini capsule with two astronauts aboard.

ROBOT EXPLORERS

Unmanned space probes have told us most of what we know about the solar system. Probes take photographs, make maps, and analyse the material that other planets are made from. They have visited all the planets except Pluto. They have also visited our Moon, the moons of other planets, the Sun, asteroids and comets.

The first probe to visit another planet was the American probe Mariner 2, which flew past Venus in 1962. Four years later, Russian Venera probes landed on the surface of Venus. In 1975 probes sent back the first pictures from the surfaces of Venus and Mars.

THE LONGEST JOURNEYS

In 1977 two Voyager probes were launched. They visited Jupiter and used its gravity to sling them on to Saturn. Voyager 2 also flew by Uranus and Neptune, where it arrived in 1989. Voyager 1 is now more than 13 billion kilometres from Earth. Both probes are still sending back data. Their radio signals take twelve hours to reach Earth.

FACT FILE

MILESTONES IN SPACE EXPLORATION

This table shows some of the most important space missions in history.

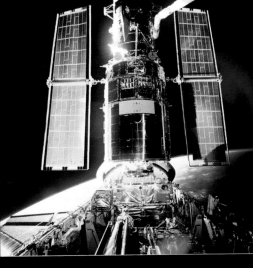

A space shuttle launching the Hubble Space Telescope.

Launch year	Craft	Mission notes
1961	Vostok 1	Took first astronaut, Yuri Gagarin, into orbit.
1962	Mariner 2	First fly-past of Venus.
1969	Apollo 11	First Moon landing.
1972/3	Pioneer 10 & 11	First fly-past of Jupiter and Saturn.
1975	Viking 1 & 2	Landed on Mars and searched for signs of life.
1977	Voyager 1 & 2	Flew past Jupiter, Saturn, Uranus and Neptune. Voyager 1 is the most remote man-made object.
1981	Columbia	First space shuttle launch.
1985	Giotto	Probe photographed Halley's Comet.
1989	Galileo	Parachuted into Jupiter's atmosphere.
1996	Pathfinder	Mars lander. Carried mini rover that moved across surface.
1997	Cassini-Huygens	Cassini orbiting Saturn. Huygens landed on Titan.
1999	Stardust	Collected dust and gas from comet Wild-2 to bring back to Earth.
2003	Spirit & Opportunity	Mars rovers.
2003	Muses-C	Japanese probe to visit asteroid and return with samples.

An artist's impression of the Huygens probe dropping towards Titan (Saturn's largest moon) in 2004.

The Moon Landings

Between 1969 and 1972 six manned spacecraft landed on the Moon, and twelve astronauts walked on the surface. They explored plains, mountains and craters, carried out dozens of experiments, and brought samples of Moon rock back to Earth.

The US Moon programme was called Apollo. Each Moon landing was a complicated mission, and there was eight years of testing and practice before Apollo 11 was ready to make the first landing. Apollo 8 made the first orbit of the Moon, testing that the spacecraft could reach the Moon and return safely. Apollo 10 was a full rehearsal, but without actually making a landing.

Eagle, separated from the command module and descended to the surface. It touched down in a flat plain called the Sea of Tranquillity. The mission commander, Neil Armstrong, climbed down Eagle's ladder and stepped on to the rocky surface, saying the famous words: 'That's one small step for a man, one giant leap for mankind.'

This diagram shows the stages of an Apollo mission. The Moon is shown three times to make the steps clearer.

WALKING ON THE MOON

On 16 July 1969, Apollo 11 blasted off for the Moon. It arrived in orbit around the Moon two days later. On 20 July the lunar module, called

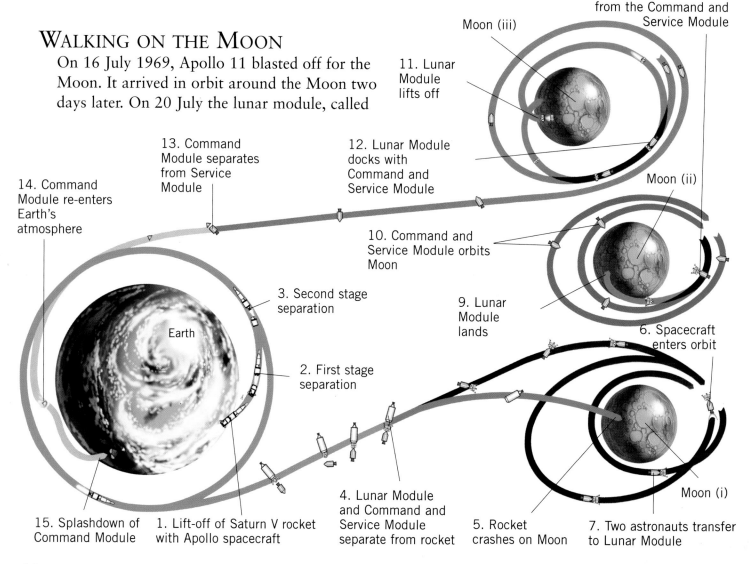

8. Lunar Module separates from the Command and Service Module

Moon (iii)

11. Lunar Module lifts off

13. Command Module separates from Service Module

12. Lunar Module docks with Command and Service Module

14. Command Module re-enters Earth's atmosphere

Moon (ii)

10. Command and Service Module orbits Moon

3. Second stage separation

Earth

9. Lunar Module lands

6. Spacecraft enters orbit

2. First stage separation

Moon (i)

15. Splashdown of Command Module

1. Lift-off of Saturn V rocket with Apollo spacecraft

4. Lunar Module and Command and Service Module separate from rocket

5. Rocket crashes on Moon

7. Two astronauts transfer to Lunar Module

38

FACT FILE

APOLLO MISSION DATA
(Mission/Landing date/Landing site/
Mission notes)

- Apollo 11
  20 July 1969
  Sea of Tranquillity
  First landing on the Moon by humans.

- Apollo 12
  19 November 1969
  Ocean of Storms
  Landed near Surveyor 3, which had
    landed 2 years before.

- Apollo 13
  (no landing)
  Oxygen tank exploded and power was
    reduced. Craft rounded Moon and
    returned, and crew were saved.

- Apollo 14
  5 February 1971
  Crater Fra Mauro
  Astronauts used a handcart to carry
    equipment and rock samples.

- Apollo 15
  30 July 1971
  Hadley Rille
  First use of a lunar rover vehicle.

- Apollo 16
  20 April 1972
  Region near crater Descartes
  Mission commander carried out speed
    and turning trials of the lunar rover.

- Apollo 17
  11 December 1972
  Near crater Littrow in Taurus mountains
  Longest Apollo mission, and the last.

**Apollo 15 on the Moon. On the right
is the lunar rover.**

The Apollo landing sites on the Moon.

MORE MISSIONS

There were six more Apollo missions after Apollo 11. Five landed successfully, each in a different spot on the near side of the Moon. The Apollo 13 mission nearly ended in disaster. There was an explosion on board on the way to the Moon, leaving the crew short of oxygen. They flew around the Moon and returned to Earth safely, using the oxygen supplies in the lunar module.

The Future

The International Space Station orbits the Earth about 400 kilometres above the surface.

This DC-XA craft was designed to replace the space shuttle, but development was cancelled.

In the early twenty-first century we are still launching robot space probes to explore the solar system for us. All the time probes are becoming more intelligent, and carrying better cameras and more sensitive testing equipment. In the future they will tell us a great deal more about our solar system.

But when will human beings travel further than the Moon? The answer is not for many years. Travelling to other planets is a long and difficult business. But in 2004 US President George Bush announced a plan to return to the Moon and to build a base there. This would be a starting point for a manned mission to Mars some time after 2020. The plan would be incredibly expensive to carry out. Some people think the money should be spent helping people on Earth instead.

An artist's impression of the first human visitors on Mars.

LIVING IN SPACE

If people ever do live on other planets in our solar system, how will they survive? This is one of the questions being answered by experiments on the International Space Station, the only place where people are living in space at the moment. Scientists aboard are investigating how people's bodies react to living in zero gravity, the effects of dangerous radiation in space, and how we could grow food on other planets.

We have a lot of exploring to do. At the moment we are just discovering the vast, unexplored region of our solar system beyond Neptune. We will find out about this strange world from the New Horizons probe, due to arrive in 2015. It will be many decades before we can leave the Earth to colonise the other planets.

 FUTURE FILE

NEW FORMS OF POWER

At the moment space probes take several years to travel to the outer solar system. Scientists are investigating new forms of power that would allow spacecraft to travel much faster than they can with rocket engines. Two possibilities are ion thrusters and solar sails. Ion thrusters send out a stream of tiny particles at high speed. Solar sails capture the solar wind, using it to very gradually speed up a spacecraft.

Death of the Solar System

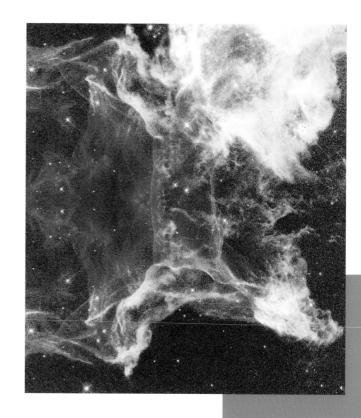

The Sun has been shining for about five billion years, and the planets have been orbiting the Sun for almost as long. Humans live for less than a hundred years, so it is hard for us to imagine the solar system coming to an end. But the Sun will not shine forever as it does today.

Astronomers think that the Sun is about halfway through its life. In another five billion years it will begin to run out of fuel. Then it will grow into a red giant star, a hundred times larger than it is today. Finally it will stop shining and die.

As our solar system dies, another may be formed in a *nebula* like this.

FUTURE FILE

THE END OF THE UNIVERSE

The universe we know was formed between 15 and 20 billion years ago. Astronomers don't know what happened before then. Neither do they know if the universe will ever come to an end. After our solar system dies, new solar systems will be born in clouds of gas and dust in other parts of the galaxy. Some stars will shine for a hundred times longer than our Sun. Eventually all the gas and dust will be used up and the galaxy will become a dark, dead place.

About 5 billion years from now, life on Earth will be destroyed by the swelling Sun.

THE END OF THE PLANETS

When the Sun grows into a red giant it will swallow up Mercury and Venus, destroying them. If the Earth's orbit grows bigger as the dying Sun loses some of its **mass**, it might escape being swallowed up too. Even if it doesn't disappear into the growing Sun, its surface will be roasted and the oceans will boil away.

THE DYING SUN

After millions of years of being a red giant, the Sun will begin to flicker slowly. When it runs out of fuel completely, its light will fade and it will shrink into an object about the size of the Earth, known as a white dwarf. The Earth and the other planets will be left as charred, cold lumps in dark space. Our solar system will be dead. Perhaps by then humans will have found a way of travelling to solar systems of younger stars, leaving our dying solar system behind.

Glossary

Asteroid A lump of rock in orbit around the Sun. Also called a minor planet.

Asteroid belt A ring of asteroids between the orbits of Mars and Jupiter.

Atmospheric pressure The pressure made by the weight of the gases in a planet's atmosphere.

Atom A very tiny particle of matter that all substances are made from.

Axis (pl. axes) The straight line around which a planet spins.

Comet A lump of dust and ice orbiting the Sun.

Constellation A pattern of stars in the night sky that resembles an imaginary animal or person.

Core The central part of a planet.

Crust The solid outer layer of a rocky planet.

Extinct Describes a species of animal or plant that has died out.

Galaxy A giant group of stars.

Gas giant A planet that is made up of substances that are normally gases on the Earth.

Gravity The force that attracts every object in the universe to every other object in the universe.

Kuiper Belt Object (KBO) An object that orbits the Sun beyond Pluto.

Light year The distance light travels in a year, equal to 9.46 million million kilometres.

Mantle The layer of the Earth underneath the thin crust. It is made up of the thin upper mantle and much thicker lower mantle.

Mass A measure of the amount of matter in an object. The units of mass are grams and kilograms.

Matter The stuff that everything in the universe is made of.

Meteor A small piece of rock or dust from space that enters the Earth's atmosphere and burns up, making a streak of light.

Meteorite A piece of rock from space that hits the ground, often making a crater.

Meteor shower A large group of meteors that hit the Earth's atmosphere. The meteors come from a comet's tail.

Molten Melted.

Nebula A giant cloud of dust and gas in space.

Nuclear fusion A nuclear reaction in which two nuclei of atoms join together, releasing energy.

Nuclear reaction When the nuclei of an atom or atoms break up or join together.

Nucleus (pl. nuclei) The central part of an atom.

Orbit The path that a planet takes as it moves around the Sun.

Probe A robot spacecraft that visits another part of the solar system.

Radar A device that uses radio waves to measure the distance to far away objects.

Radiation Any form of energy that travels as electromagnetic waves (such as light and radio waves) or a stream of particles.

Ringlets Narrow rings around a planet that together make up larger rings.

Satellite An object that orbits another object in space.

Solar system A group of planets and moons and the star that they orbit.

Solar wind A stream of electronically-charged particles that blows outwards from the Sun.

Sub-atomic particle Any particle of matter that is smaller than an atom.

Sunspot A cool, dark patch on the surface of the Sun.

Tectonic plates The giant sections that the Earth's crust is cracked into.

Further Information

PLACES TO VISIT

The British Astronomical Association
Britain's senior astronomical society for amateur astronomers. Membership open to everybody.
British Astronomical Association, Burlington House, Piccadilly, London W1J 0DU
www.britastro.org

The Society for Popular Astronomy
Astronomy society with plenty of advice and guidance for beginners. Membership open to everybody.
Society for Popular Astronomy
36 Fairway, Keyworth, Nottingham NG12 5DU
www.popastro.com

BOOKS TO READ

Look into Space: Our Solar System by Jon Kirkwood (Franklin Watts, 2002)
Looking at Stars: Night Sky/Planets/Stars and Galaxies/Sun by Robin Kerrod (Chrysalis, 2001)
Science Quest: Space by Robert Sneddon (Chrysalis, 2003)
The Best Ever Book of Astronomy by Carole Stott (Kingfisher, 2003)
The Kingfisher Book of Space by Martin Redfern (Kingfisher, 1998)

WEBSITES

http://www.nasa.gov
The home page of NASA. Loads of information, images and activities about the solar system and space travel.

http://www.bbc.co.uk/science/space
This BBC website contains lots of information on all aspects of space, as well as space-related activities.

http://www.nssc.co.uk
The home page of the UK's National Space Centre.

http://mystarslive.com
A website that draws a map of the night sky viewed from where you live. Good for finding the planets.

Index

The Universe (30 billion light years across; 1 light year = 9.46 trillion km/5.88 trillion mi)

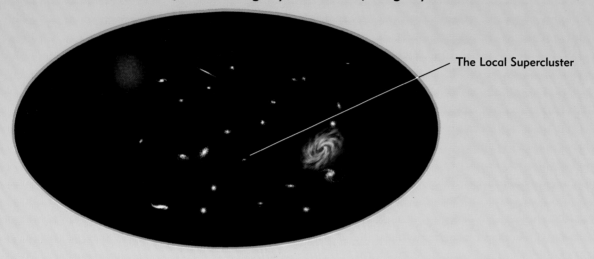

The Local Supercluster

The Local Supercluster (100 million light years across)

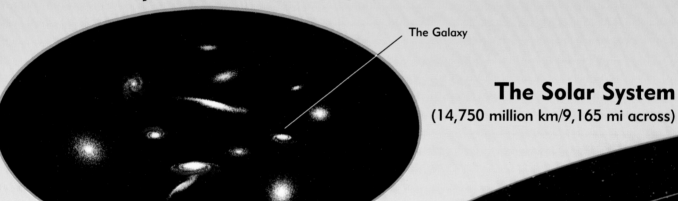

The Galaxy

The Solar System
(14,750 million km/9,165 mi across)

The Galaxy (100,000 light years across)

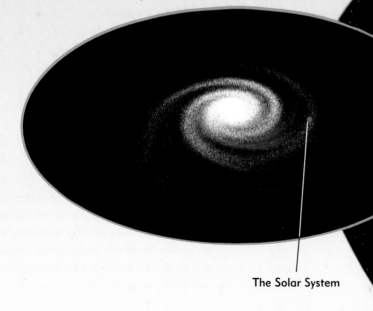

The Solar System